Before telephones were decriminalized, a tour of San Francisco was not complete without a surreptitious visit to the sinister underground "telephone dens." Here addicts spent endless hours talking with relatives in Oakland.

The Phony Phone Book

Scads and oodles of new wonderful ways
to answer your telephone, well calculated to earn you a reputation
for originality, wittiness and a nice voice,
together with hitherto-undisclosed facts about the secret history and sex life
of your indispensable communication instrument.

Written, punctuated and graphically enhanced (with pictures) by

Milford ("Stanley") Poltroon

Winchester Press

Important Notice:

Cloning of this book [or reproduction by any other method] is forbidden, except by mating it with any other book by Milford Poltroon and assuming full responsibility for the offspring. Also, apperceptive book reviewers may quote from the cuddly contents to their Heart's Content, as part of swell book reviews; likewise radio and TV "personalities."

Contact the publishers for the smash motion picture rights.

Other Works by Milford ("Stanley") Poltroon

How To Fish Good
The Happy Fish Hooker
The Wretched Mess Calendar
Hi-Middle-Low Moosepoker

The brave men who strung our nation's first telephone lines had nerves of steel.

Library of Congress Cataloging in Publication Data

Poltroon, Milford.
  The phony phone book.

  1. Telephone etiquette—Anecdotes, facetiae, satire,
etc. 2. Telephone—Anecdotes, facetiae, satire,
etc. I. Title.
PN6231.T5P6   818'.5'407   79-454
ISBN 0-87691-280-3
9 8 7 6 5 4 3 2 1

Published by Winchester Press
205 East 42nd Street
New York, New York 10017

WINCHESTER is a Trademark of Olin Corporation, used by Winchester Press, Inc. under authority and control of the Trademark Proprietor

Printed in the United States of America

DINGALING

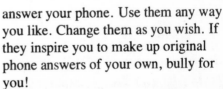

This book shows you oodles of dandy new ways to answer your telephone.

The telephone was invented in 1876. But since then, people have learned only 3 ways to respond, when the bell goes ringy-dingy:

1. They say "Hello," the most overworked word in the English language.
2. They recite their name. Like "Ormly Gumfudgin speaking." Except no one else has a name as interesting as Ormly Gumfudgin.*
3. They recite their phone number. Like "339-0000." This is not very exciting.

Something better is needed.

Back in 1905, the phone company, aware of this problem, tried to solve it with this paragraph in phone directories:

HOW TO ANSWER THE TELEPHONE

Remove the hand telephone and say "HERE IS MAIN 297" (or whatever their number may be). The party calling should then say "THIS IS MAIN 298" (or whatever their number may be). Much friction and annoyance will be avoided if this simple plan is carried out.

Despite its simplicity, the plan never made it.

This book, however, offers you not just one, but an enormous mess of ways to answer your phone. Use them any way you like. Change them as you wish. If they inspire you to make up original phone answers of your own, bully for you!

When you answer your phone in a truly original way, you'll find that most callers will promptly hang up in total bewilderment. The time you thus save, in avoiding inane conversations, will soon more than pay for the cost of this book (too cheap).

*Ormly Gumfudgin is a real person who writes a column for some southern California newspapers. He is also a friend of mine. And I will fight the man who says it isn't so.

Foreword

Ever since I was first bewitched by the wit and charm of this book's author, I knew we had several things in common:

1. Creative people are to be kept in the kitchen—like the great chefs of the world—and never allowed to mingle with the customer.

2. Creative people fully understand the beneficial effects that Jack Daniel's has on the creative juices.

3. Creative people know that the genuine Bell telephone is the world's greatest invention; and Bell Yellow Pages a strong second place contender (for it tells you Who, What, Where, When and Why).

I first met Milford ("Stanley") Poltroon when Pacific Northwest Bell was looking for an advertising agency. This was back in 1960—when a long-distance call from San Francisco to New York cost $2.25 for three minutes. (Today the same call costs $1.30 when you dial it yourself.)

When ("Stanley") and his famed agency (Guild, Bascom and Bonfigli) gave us their pitch, a salient fact emerged: If we were to retain them as our agency, we were indeed opting to run advertising that would be striking out in a new direction. Like ("Stanley"), it was going to be different—as were the people on the account. ("Stanley") assuaged our concern at being too different by pointing out that Seattle was some 3,000 miles from the home office. "They'll never see or hear anything about your advertising way out here," said he.

He was dead wrong on that score. Our advertising was different. The Madison Avenue in-term for it was "off-beat, but on-beat." In this pursuit we tried new things. Tim Conway, Phyllis Diller, Max Morath, and Bill "my name José Jiménez" Dana were some of the then-unknown personalities we used in our advertising. Our "New Yorker's idea of the United States" map was a big hit. As was our "Let's tell the world about Washington/Oregon" tourism promotional campaign.

Those were fun years. But not without some growing pains from my good friend ("Stanley"). He tossed Pacific Telephone into a quandary with his own personal communications problem, when he asked that his upright black phone be placed on his desk. Problem: The desk sat on a turntable that rotated.

Then there was his suggestion that we give each phone customer a bottle of Jack Daniel's with every bill. Thinking being: If it worked on the average customer as it did on him, we would enjoy a tremendous boost in long-distance calling on late evenings or early mornings when the telephone circuitry was more relaxed. As was ("Stanley").

And we loved his idea of blasting out a hunk of Mt. Rainer to erect a bust of Alexander Graham Bell. Larger, of course, than that of the other mortals of Mt. Rushmore.

Another of his winners was explaining to us how he thought the Nobel prize was named. ("Stanley") claimed it followed right after A. G. Bell brought his phone to the patent office, and was told, "No, Bell."

Which reminds me, this book is a No Bell product, as it has not been endorsed in any way, shape, or form by the Bell System. The kisses and/or barbs tossed at various units of our company are either totally unfounded or ridiculously true as the case may be.

But on the personal side, the book can enhance immeasurably your own phone enjoyment with the new wonderful ways to answer the telephone. And I suggest that the more lengthy responses be especially used when someone is calling you long distance. And while I'm suggesting, let me also suggest that each of you should sit down after reading this book and write out your own long-winded greetings to be used when calling someone. Especially on long-distance calls.

And now, before you sit back and enjoy ("Stanley") at his best, let me share with you some of his philosophy. Heretofore never revealed: The system is the solution. You can Be Choosy in selecting your own genuine Bell phone complete with custom calling services at one of our PhoneCenter Stores. You then will be able to reach out and touch someone you love by long distance. It's the next best thing to being there.

Dan E. Hutchins
Advertising Director
American Telephone & Telegraph Co.

For David Bentley Tolls

Notice:

All the facts contained in this book are 100% true,
except for those that are not.

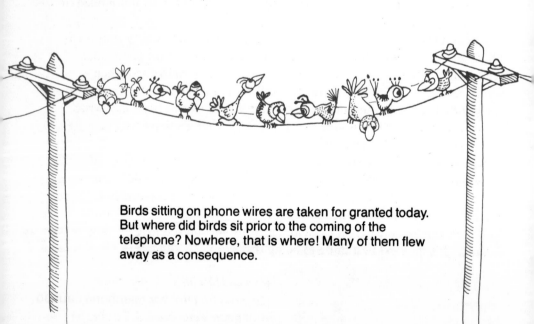

Birds sitting on phone wires are taken for granted today.
But where did birds sit prior to the coming of the
telephone? Nowhere, that is where! Many of them flew
away as a consequence.

The Phony Phone Book

BEFORE

AFTER

Can Telephones Cause Loss of Hair?

Shortly after phone service came to Utica, Pennsylvania, Mr. Henry Mushrush of that city complained that frequent use of his telephone caused his hair to fall out. The phone company refused comment.

There you are in the bathroom when the phone rings . . .

I was sitting in my bathroom,
   When the phone rang down the hall;
I was forced to move with unseemly haste
   In order to answer its call.
So now that I've been unseated,
   Please make your words short and sweet;
And kindly don't dilly or dally;
   I've another call to complete.

I'm talking from my bathroom,
I hope that you're not minding;
And I prefer not to talk
About anything that's binding.

A pair of bedroom phone answers...

I'm talking here from my bedroom,
With the covers pulled over my head.
  I'm still half asleep,
  So don't give me no bleep,
Or I'll kick you out of my bed.

I'm here in the arms of Morpheus,
  We're together here in the sack;
And I don't feel like talking now,
  So can I call you back?

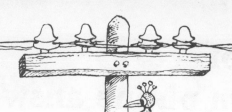

Phone answers appropriate for use under the specific circumstances described . . .

The phone rang as I went by
    jogging,
I've gone forty times round the
    block!
I'll be good for six more
To add to my score,
After you finish your talk.

I've been out exercising my frisbee;
    When the phone rang, I threw it
    up high!
Speak briefly so I can catch it
    When it comes down from the
    sky.

I'm about to sit down to my
    breakfast;
    Two eggs are calling to me.
My coffee and toast,
    They both want me the most
So avoid all verbosity.

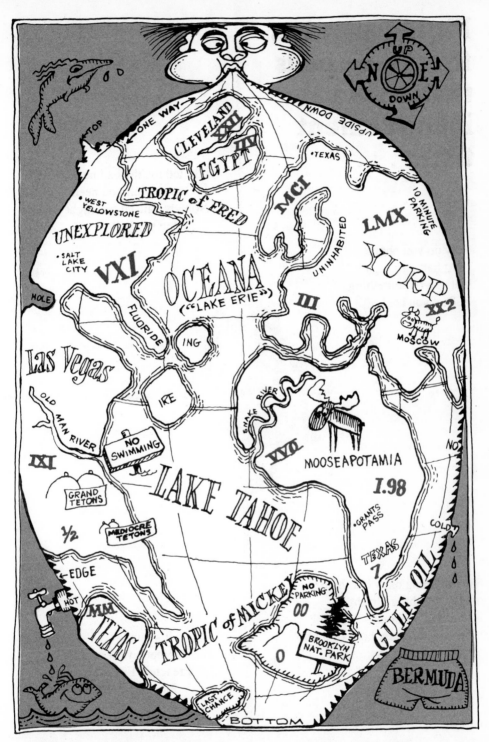

Ancient pre-Christian era map of the world, divided by area codes

Fitting answers for phone calls that arrive at inconvenient times . . .

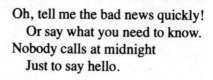

Oh, tell me the bad news quickly!
   Or say what you need to know.
Nobody calls at midnight
   Just to say hello.

Why do you phone
   At half past eight?
Is it maybe something
   That you ate?

Is everything okay out there?
   Is everything alright?
If so, whyja phone
   At this ungodly hour of night?

So it's Sunday,
   What's your sermon?
Preach in English,
   Please, no German.

A phone answer deemed appropriate if one receives a call while dining in a German restaurant . . .

A knockwurst is sitting
In my sauerkraut.
Now what did you want
To talk about?

A phone answer quite fitting if one has just returned from the Debutante's Ball . . .

In '07, Auguste and Pierre Gonzales became the first men to cross the Atlantic in an open telephone.

I've just come back
From the Debutante's Ball,
So what's the reason
For your call?

15

Phone answers pertinent to particular places . . .

You've reached me here in Tennessee,
My homage here is annual;
I come to lay a rose upon
The grave of old Jack Daniel.

I'm waiting now
To hear your voice,
Here in Chicago,
Illinois.

You may tittle,
You may tattle.
It's raining up here
In Seattle.

Eminent professors at Bell Laboratories
continually study new ways of improving
the telephone. Here a group discusses
possible hole enlargement in phone dials,
for people with chubby fingers.

A phone answer appropriate for April 15 . . .

Please avoid
   All supplication;
It's all gone
   After taxation.

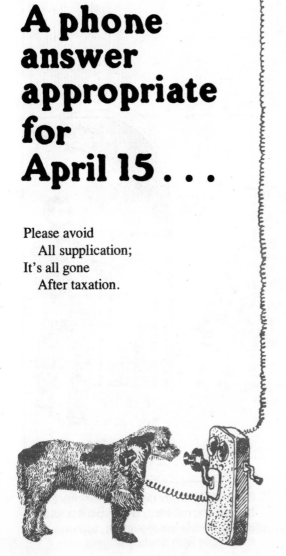

I'm speaking to you from
      the clinic,
   I'm here for excess gas.
I hope the words you're
      about to speak
   Will cause no more to pass.

Alexander Graham Bell demonstrated his first telephone at the World Exhibition in Philadelphia, in 1876. Its size, approximating that of a steamer trunk, moved spectators to exclaim, "That's a big mother, Bell!" So it was that the telephone company gained the affectionate name by which we know it today.

A suitable phone answer, if one suspects the caller is about to ask to take your helpmeet on a piscatorial peregrination, and one wishes to refuse . . .

If you called to ask permission
To take my wife out fishin',
The answer is
No,
Joe.

The opposite of the preceding, this phone answer enables one to graciously accede to a request for one's spouse to engage in sport with rod and reel . . .

If you phoned to ask permish
For Roy to go catch fish,
The answer is
Yes,
Jess.

A phone answer suitable for anyone harboring an interest in deciduous trees . . .

The male offspring of beech trees,
Our silviculture teaches,
Are commonly referred to
As little sons of beeches.
To expand my store of knowledge
Is my constant aim;
So, dear sir or madam,
Pray tell me, what's your name?

Reindeer were used to haul in equipment when telephone service was introduced to Siberia. However, telephones never "caught on," because the Russians proved unable to think up a good area code for the place.

A straight-from-the-shoulder phone answer to use if one suspects the caller may be an ingrained horse thief . . .

I'm telling you straight,
  Right here on this phone,
You better leave
  My horse alone.

Roger Brashears, a farmer living near Tullahoma, Tennessee, claimed to have a phone that ate carrots, shortly after phone service came to that area. "Rosie and I don't dare leave carrots out in the open, or that darn telephone eats 'em all up." An investigator from the phone company said the story was greatly exaggerated. "The phone eats mostly parsley," he reported.

Phone answers highly appropriate for the particular circumstances mentioned . . .

If you're calling from the bank to say
  That I am overdrawn,
There's no one at this number.
  Or at least, I'll soon be gone.

You're calling to say
  That I have won
The Irish Sweepstakes, yes?
  Well, rush the money,
Honey!
  I'm in a financial mess.

23

Insults and

My telephone went ringy-ding,
  So I took it from the hook.
I hope this call's intelligent
  And that you are not a schnook.

Speak up! Do not hesitate!
  You may now confabulate!
I hope your head is screwed on straight
  And that I don't regurgitate.

What is it that
  You want to know?
Are you a klutz
  Or just a schmoe?

An unsuccessful attempt to invent a
telephone was made by Victor Kowalski in
1832. The instrument employed the shell
of a marine bivalve as a listening device.
The mouthpiece, however, caused users
to expire from asphyxiation.

Semi-insults

A meeting of minds
   May now be expedient,
Providing you have
   The essential ingredient.

If what you say
   Proves to be boring,
You will hear me
   Softly snoring.

If you bring good tidings
   I will love it!
Otherwise, take your phone
   And shove it.

In my chair I'll
   Sit and swivel
While I listen
   To your drivel.

Another unsuccessful attempt to invent a telephone was made by Luigi Buccello in 1849.

A quartet of phone answers wherein the caller is warned that you will tolerate no balderdash . . .

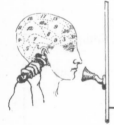

Give me gently
   Your harangue,
Or up is what
   I will hang.

You may talk,
   If you're inclined to.
I'll listen, if I
   Have a mind to.

If your words
   Will make me nervous,
Then this phone
   Is not in service.

I hold my phone to my good ear
   So that your voice I now may hear,
But if I don't like this interview
   Then I will hang up on you.

Tom Swift and his Steam Telephone

Eschewing the expensive batteries used by other telephones in the early 1900s, the intrepid young inventor created an instrument with power supplied entirely by the person making the call. A novel feature permitted the caller to fly the telephone directly to one's home if one's line was busy.

More

You're connected to the number
That you have tried to reach,
So now I'll have to listen
To your jabberwocky speech.

Altho my crock's
Already full,
I'll listen while
You shoot the bull.

Insults . . .

I'll listen now
    To your flapdoodle;
I hope that you're
    Not off your noodle.

Please avoid all
    Incredulity
As I endure your
    Garrulity.

I'll submit to
    Your verbosity;
Give it to me
    With velocity.

Alexander Graham Beep
Inventor of the sound one hears if one's
telephone conversation is being
recorded.

GREAT PHONE BOOTHS OF HISTORY #219
The Pornophone

This innovative instrument made it possible for one to make a phone call while simultaneously viewing a porno movie. Its inventor, an inspector on the Hoboken vice squad, postulated that perverts fond of making obscene phone calls would be attracted by public Pornophones, where they could be easily apprehended by vigilant police. To their chagrin, officers found Pornophones were used mostly by insurance men and investment counselors.

A fitting phone answer if one wishes to determine the skin pigmentation of the caller, albeit incurring the risk of being accused of racism . . .

Roses are red
   Violets are blue
Do you mind if I ask
   What color are you?

I've heard the birds in my garden
   The frogs in my little brook, too;
I've heard the soft breeze
   As it rustles the leaves,
So now must I listen to YOU?

In the world's 1st successful
telephone transplant, Benny
Frankel of Tucson, Arizona,
had an operative phone dial
implanted in his stomach.
Instead of a bell to signal
incoming calls, his stomach
rumbled.

Compliments and Kind Words

You're very smart.
You deserve a raise.
Did you call to hear
This sincere praise?

You have impressive eyebrows
And a dimple on your chin,
You're a sparkling conversationalist,
So why don't you begin?

Today you're looking
Ten years younger!
Is this maybe
Caused by hunger?

More Compliments and Kind Words

You're looking good!
  You've lost some weight!
Did you call to ask me
  For a date?

I like your haircut!
  It's becoming!
When you speak
  Then I'll start humming.

I'm glad you called!
  Hot diggety dog!
Shall we have
  A dialogue?

The famous drive-through telephone in Yosemite National Park.

A phone answer well calculated to discourage unnecessary conversation . . .

I think that they got this phone bugged,
   I think someone is listening in;
So think very careful what you have to say
   Before you commence to begin.
It could be those FBI sneakies
   Or maybe the CIA,
So maybe you better just not say a thing
   Or they might take us away.

poltroon

Phone answers deliberately designed to discourage long-winded hangers-on . . .

I'm about to sit down to my dinner,
  And I don't want my food to get cold.
So avoid all superfluous verbiage,
  As you tell me what has to be told.

My dishwasher's flooding the
    kitchen,
  And my cat is chasing my birds;
My dog caught his tail in the wringer,
  So please don't use any long words.

I'm ready to leave for the airport
  And I can't be late for my plane;
I've got to be there when it takes to the air,
  From long speeches I hope you'll
    refrain.

Some burglars are smashing my windows,
    And the back of my house is on fire;
There are bats flying out of my chimney,
    So say quickly what you require.

Say quickly what
    You have to say;
They're waiting outside
    To take me away.

The advent of the telephone and its
accompanying transmission lines made
rescuing of damsels in distress
considerably easier.

Phone answers well calculated to encourage clear articulation and to discourage wishy-washy language . . .

Don't mumble or stammer
Or use obscure prose;
Speak clearly, distinctly,
And not through your nose.

Try not to squeak
And do not shriek,
And I'll listen
As you speak.

Keep your language
In sharp focus,
Don't give me any
Hocus-pocus.

Speak distinctly, state your case;
Say your words, then shut your face.

Do not mumble,
Do not lisp, or
In my ear you
May not whisper.

Don't speak to me
In gobbledygook,
Or up is what
I will be shook.

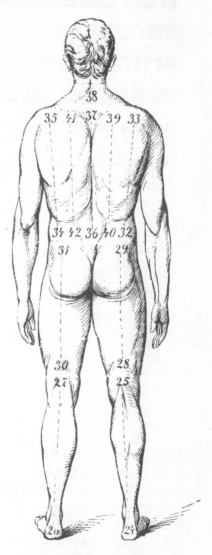

When telephones first came into use, it was deemed fashionable to have one's telephone number tattooed onto one's body. Wealthy clam magnate Maynard Shake of Boston was the first man to have 14 telephones.

If the news
    You're going to cater,
Feed me headlines;
    Details later.

I'm ready now
    To hear your lecture.
Just the facts, please;
    No conjecture.

More phone answers to discourage prolixity . . .

I'm listening, I'm waiting,
    My breath I am bating,
I can't wait to hear what you say!
    I shiver my liver,
So come on, deliver!
    I just can't wait here all day!

Please don't be loquacious,
    My time's worth a lot.
Extremely linguacious
    I hope you are not.

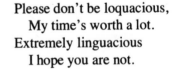

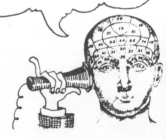

A phone answer suitable for retirement home residents . . .

Darling, I am growing old,
  Silver threads among the gold;
But ere I finally go my way,
  Hurry, what have you to say?

Hesitation
  And procrastination
Are enemies
  Of conversation.
SPEAK UP!

The Fake Snake Phone

When phone service first became available, the advertising agency thought a fake snake, leaping from the mouth of the telephone, would help popularize the instrument. However, this proved to be a wrong number.

An effective phone answer for use when you are in no mood to tolerate nervous giggles . . .

A pair of phone answers that champion pithy prose and oppose ambiguity . . .

You may commence
  Your phone oration,
But please avoid
  All titteration.

My phone rang with lucidity,
  I answered with rapidity;
So speak with pellucidity
  And please eschew vapidity,
And especially,
  Stupidity.

Now that you've
  Got my attention,
What is it that you
  Want to mention?

FIRST PHONE DIRECTORY
In the early days of the telephone, the ad agency believed phone directories should have catchy titles and contain information on food, beverage and sex preferences of subscribers, as well as their telephone numbers and astrological signs. It was learned the books could be simplified.

43

A phone answer offering money-saving nutritionally sound advice if one suspects the caller may be overspending on his or her food budget . . .

Okra, turnips, rice and beans
 Help one live within their means.
Instead of steak, try cheese soufflé;
 Now tell me what you have to say.

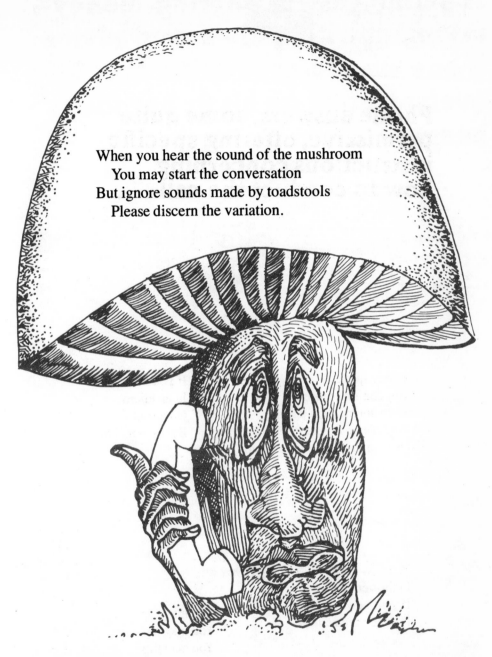

When you hear the sound of the mushroom
   You may start the conversation
But ignore sounds made by toadstools
   Please discern the variation.

(This phone answer takes advantage of the fact that only one person in 817 knows that sounds made by mushrooms and toadstools are *identical*; both are below the thresholds of normal human hearing and are audible only to other mushrooms and toadstools.)

Phone answers, some quite permissive, offering specific instructions concerning how to conduct the call...

  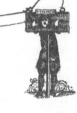

You may speak
  But don't be prolix,
And do not mention politics.
  And please do not discuss religion.
So how are you, my little pigeon?

If you must speak
In an idiom
Go ahead
But do not kiddium.

You may speak
In the vernacular
If your news
Is quite spectacular.

You may yap.
You may rap.
You may flip
And I will flap.

If you speak foreign, please hang up;
    My ears are programmed for English
        only.
So don't give me no parley-voos,
    And don't feed me Italian baloney.

Start at the beginning
    And finish at the end.
Now proceed to tell me
    What's your problem, friend?

You may talk
You may sing,
Because my phone went
Ringy-ding!

In the heyday of vaudeville, one of the
most popular acts was Horace and Esther
Scrodd ("The Phonatics"), who
performed all manner of merry stunts with
telephones.

An appropriate phone answer, if one is adept at imitating Groucho Marx

Hello, hello, hello, hello!
Hello, hello, hello!
To start our conversation,
I'll say hello, hello!
But I cannot stay
The livelong day,
And shortly I must go.
But before I say goodbye, I'll say
Hello, hello, hello!

A phone answer suitable for Al Jolson impersonators

Hello, mah baby! Hello, mah honey!
Hello, mah ragtime gal!
Hello there, whoever you are!
Is this Hal, Cal, Sal or Al?

The 4-cylinder Dial-A-Cycle, invented by Harley Suzuki, enabled cyclists to call home to mother while en route.

BEFORE   **AFTER**

Can Telephones Help Overcome Baldness?

Six months after telephone service came to Eagle Point, Oregon, Mr. T. G. Staley of that city claimed frequent use of the telephone caused all his hair to grow back in again. Pacific Northwest Bell generously agreed not to charge extra for this service.

A phone answer for those capable of performing an impression of Mr. Phil Harris

You are speaking to the party
To whom you are connected.
I'm the one that you've selected
For your voice to be directed
At, and you may speak in confidence,
Your words will be protected!
And that's what I like about the South!
HELLO!

Milestones in Telephone History

In 1889, telephone listening parlours were opened to the public in naughty Paris. People were offered a choice of things they might listen to:

French chef explaining how to boil clams	1 franc
How to find the Men's Room in the Louvre	2 francs
Nose flautist rehearsals, Opera House	2 francs
Sound of egg, thrown from top of Eiffel Tower, landing on crowd below	3 francs
Oriental customer telling French laundry how to do his shirts	2 francs
Obscene phone call	1 franc

Animal lovers, naturalists and those fond of imitating the sounds of domestic fauna will find the following phone answers to their taste . . .

Doggie say WOOF!
  Kitty say MEOW!
I'm waiting to hear
  What you say now.

Cow say MOO!
  Horsie say NEIGH!
So what do you
  Have to say?

Duck go QUACK!
  Train go TOOT!
Is you an owl?
  Okay: HOOT!

A phone answer for any person adept at imitating horse sounds . . .

When you hear the sound of the horse
  You may start in to talk;
But have no fear, and do not rear,
  Or whinny, shy or balk.

(Follow immediately with your horse impression.)

51

Junk Calls

If you're a salesman
And not a friend,
This phone call's
Coming to an end.

**Phone answers
if one
intuitively
knows the
caller is going
to try to sell
something . . .**

Oh, what are you trying to peddle?
What are you trying to sell?
I just know you are some kind of
    salesman,
By the sound of my telephone bell.
So recite your memorized sales talk,
But no matter what you may say,
Just understand this clearly:
I don't want any today.

If you called to sell me insurance,
Or peddle some real estate,
You're wasting your time
I don't have a dime,
So I cannot swallow your bait.

If you called to sell me something,
    Benny,
The fact is I do not want any.

An effective phone answer if one somehow senses that the caller is intent on selling a hippopotamus . . .

I like gooses
I love mooses
But I don't want
No hippopotamooses.

A phone answer certain to bring results if the owner of the hippopotamus persists in his or her attempt to sell same . . .

I've just been reading
War and Peace,
And I don't want
Any hippopotameese.*

*While this phone answer admittedly makes use of a non sequitur, authoritative research proves that fewer than one hippopotamus purveyor in 87 ever notices it.

Phone answers that help fight crime!

Keep thy tongue
from evil
And thy lips from
speaking guile;
If you heed this
admonition,
You may speak
with me a while.

A phone answer appropriate for use by police officers and members of the clergy . . .

Speak up, please,
But use discretion;
I'm ready to hear
Your full confession.

A phone answer recommended if one suspects the caller is about to embark on a lifetime of crime . . .

I'll listen to what
You have to say,
But first let me tell you:
CRIME DOES NOT PAY!

What mischief would thou
Now contrive?
I'm prepared to hear
Your shrive.*

*Not 1 person in 27 knows that shrive means confession. But now you do. This shows how this swell book helps to up your culture.

When you suspect the caller has called the wrong number . . .

This ain't Duffy's Tavern,
   Or Harry's Bar and Grill;
It's not the bowling alley
   Or Doctor Liverpill.
It ain't the welfare center
   So if you're calling one of those
You got the wrong number
   Because you dialed wrong,
      I suppose.

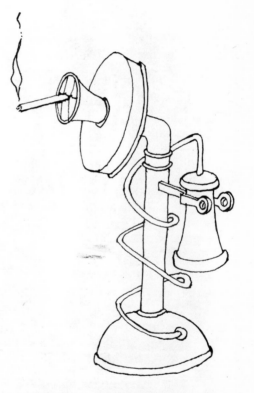

The number you have tried to reach
Is not viable.
To reach the party that you wished
You're not liable.

Roses are red
Crabgrass is umber
I surely hope
This is not a wrong number.

In the early days of telephones, a dentist in Wilderville, Oregon, claimed to have a phone that smoked cigarettes, sometimes up to two packs a day. "It isn't enough that it should stink, it coughs so much my patients won't use it," he complained to the phone company. They ultimately replaced the instrument.

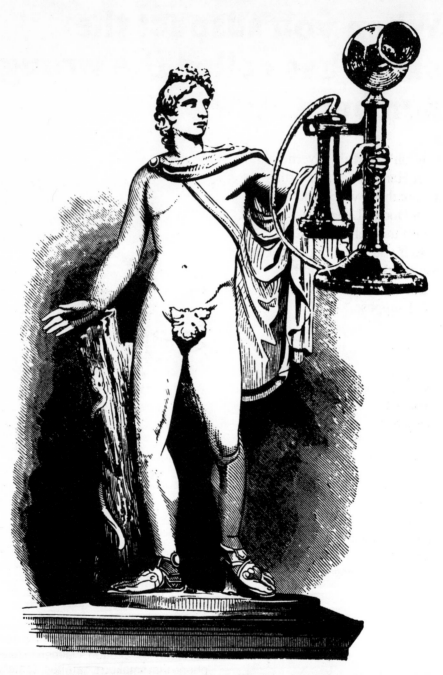

Shortly after telephones were introduced in the late 1800s, word spread that use of the instruments could cause the dread Figleaf Rash. The concerned telephone company promptly built Figleaf Rash Suppressors into all its instruments.

Apt answers to various solicitations & invitations

If you called to try to collect a bill,
   Try my office in Brazil,
Or phone my yacht club in Siberia
   Now you may speak, but I may not
      hear ya.

If you called to invite me to dinner,
   And afterwards, maybe a show,
The answer, I guess,
      is probably "yes,"
   Otherwise, absolutely it's "no."

A genteel yet forceful phone answer to use if one suspects the caller is about to ask permission to run a cattle drive through one's living room . . .

Yippie Eye Ki Yay!
It's a wonderful sort of a day!
But keep your cows out of my living
      room.
So what else do you have to say?

57

Phone Answers For the

Would you believe it is now Christmas eve?
In my chimney a fat man is stuck!
Outside my front door, people singing galore;
You're calling to add to this shuck?

Deck the halls
With boughs of holly!
I hope this call
Is full of jolly.

May your New Year
Be propitious!
That for you
Is what I wishes.

Yuletide Season . . .

I hope your New Year's happy,
   And full of peachy stuff!
If you don't wish me likewise,
   I'm leaving in a huff.

A trio of phone answers suitable for use on Mr. Washington's natal day . . .

Today's the birthday of a man
   Who never told a lie.
I hope you'll now do likewise,
   Or at any rate, please try.

If they put your picture on a stamp,
Wouldn't that light up your lamp?
And maybe on some money, too?
If George could do it, why not you?

Today is Georgie's birthday.
   He always told the truth.
And bananas grow in Iceland.
   Are you phoning from a booth?

More Phone Answers for Holidays . . .

EASTER

There's a chicken in my garden
That looks just like a bunny
But bunnies, they do not lay eggs;
Explain that to me honey.

Are you calling to wish me a greeting
Because it's the day of the bunny?
You're bringing me maybe a purple egg?
Or better yet, lovely green money?

THANKSGIVING

This is the day to be thankful
For our blessings, in effect;
Like your thoughtfulness in phoning me
But not doing it collect.

To the phone I just came
Wobble wobble
To listen to you
Gobble gobble.

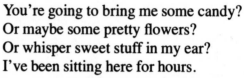

A Valentine Trio of Phone Answers . . .

You're going to bring me some candy?
Or maybe some pretty flowers?
Or whisper sweet stuff in my ear?
I've been sitting here for hours.

On this call
    You spent a dime,
Because today
    Is Valentine?

This is the day
    For Mr. Cupid.
I hope you don't say
    Nothing stupid.

And a pair for your very own birthday . . .

Did you call to offer
To help me blow
Out the candles on my birthday cake?
Three fire trucks are
Standing by;
It's just a precaution I take.

Today's my birthday!
Start to dish me
Whatever it is
You want to wish me.

63

Milestones in Telephone History

In 1880, sounds of four men eating cheeseburgers in Passaic, New Jersey, were heard distinctly by Mrs. Lulu Bascom in her home, over 17 miles away. Prior to this time, telephones had been used for voice communication only.

A phone answer appropriate for use just before election day . . .

If you called to tell me
    How to vote,
Please start rowing
    In your boat;
Up your creek
    Or up your bay,
And come back after
    Election day.

And one for Halloween . . .

You're phoning to tell me
Trick or treat?
To dress like a ghost
Did you take a sheet?

Right Foot of a Telephone Company Vice-President

1. Tibia. 2. Astragal. 3. Heel-bone. 4. Navicular. 5. Internal cuneiform bone. 6. First meta-tarsal. 7, 8. Phalanges of great toe. 9. Inferior ligament. 10. Plantar fascia, supporting the plantar arch. 11. Achilles tendon.

Shorties

Hey there, Minnie!
What's the skinny?

You may converse
In prose or verse.

Go ahead
Bat the fat.
Please tell me
Where it's at.

Whether you're
Chinese or Russian
You may now
Start the discussion.

So what's the news
In Timbuktoos?

Well, shrink my hemorrhoidal
tissue!
This is me. I hope this issue!

My telephone went tinkle, tinkle;
Is this you, Isadore Garfinkle?

I'll listen now
To your discourse
Even if you're
Part of a horse.

Hello there,
You lovely thing!
Why did you cause
My phone to ring?

What's the word?
Sing it, bird!

Gimme the scoop,
Shoot the poop.

Hear ya talkin'!
Start in rockin'!

Be you nobleman
Or rabble,
I will listen to
Your babble.

I sit here
In my BVDs,
Waiting for you
To bat the breeze.

Whether you're
A him or her,
You may commence now
To confer.

Hey! Hey!
Whattaya say?

Hang up, beat it, go away,
I'm not answering phones
today.

Bertha, Opal, Tina, Lizzie,
Please don't call me
when I'm busy.

More Shorties

An answer for nursery rhyme lovers . . .

Fee fie fo fang
My phone just rang.

Fiddle de dum
Fiddle de dee,
What is it that
You want of me?

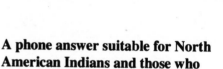

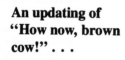

I've just
Finished flushin'
So start
The discussion.

A phone answer suitable for North American Indians and those who emulate their customs . . .

How now!
Pow wow!

An updating of "How now, brown cow!" . . .

How's the scene,
Brown bovine?

I'll now audition
Your petition.

A phone answer that acknowledges the fact that phone lines are essential to telephone communications, yet not discriminating against other species of lines . . .

In this great big world of ours
   There are many kinds of lines;
Fishing, clothes, hair and nose,
   Straight, pug and aquiline.
There are boundary lines and party lines
   Fence and timber, too;
But my favorite is this phone line,
   Connecting me with you.

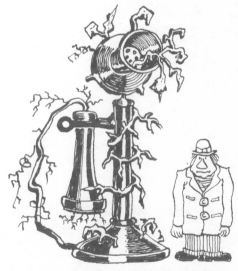

Because early day phones were made from organic materials, they would often take root and grow, if kept in a damp place. Mr. Samuel Weill of North Waterford, Maine, grew a telephone over 11 feet tall. All modern phones are made with Growth Inhibitors.

69

Milestones in Telephone History

In 1878, Chicago police began using strategically placed telephones to report accidents. Here a police wagon hurries to the aid of a man who injured himself by walking into a phone booth.

71

There are bells on cows
And bells on doors
And in churches, far and near;
There's our Liberty Bell
And evening bells,
That ring out, loud and clear.
Fire bells and Christmas bells,
And the Hell's Belles that I've known,
But the bell that now brought
You to me,
Is on my telephone.

The Raven
by Edgar Allan Areacode

Once upon a midnight dreary, as I pondered weak and weary,
Over many a quaint and curious volume of yellow pages lore—
While I nodded, earlobes swinging, suddenly there came a ringing
As of something dingalinging, ringing near my chamber door.
So hey there, bird! What's the word?

The moving finger dials, and having dialed,
Hangs loose. Nor all thy piety nor wit
Shall lure it back to cancel out a digit
Nor all your tears wash out an area code.

What the world has been waiting for—

Answers to Obscene Calls . . .

Can't you think
  Of better things to do—
Like visiting your mother
  At the zoo?

Your vocabulary's limited;
In fact, it seems so small
If you didn't use four-letter words
You couldn't talk at all.

You'd surely excite
  My sex hunger
If I were only
  80 years younger.

The funny things you're saying—
I don't know what they mean,
Because I'm not a person,
I'm an answering machine.

Phone answers to heavy breathers . . .

Here speaks Moira Ditzel Levy;
Oi, what makes your breath so heavy?

Oh, I'm so glad you called again!
I was bored to death!
But now you're on the phone again;
It's nice to hear your breath.

If the cat has got your tongue,
Tell me, why has my phone rung?

A "wireless" telephone invented during the Millard Fillmore administration proved surprisingly effective if the caller was not more than 4 feet from the callee.

A young man whose name was Depew
Kept a phone in his barbecue;
All the calls that he got
Proved exceedingly hot,
Which he answered by yelling "YAHOOOOOO!"

An old man from Kalamazoo
Had a phone in his private zoo;
When the instrument rang
He got a bang
Out of saying "Hello there, what's gnu?"

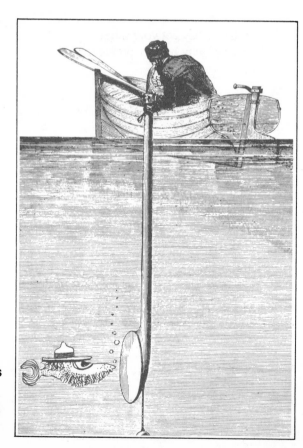

Invented by Professor Wilbur Smirk, the Bass-O-Phone enabled one to listen to largemouth bass talking in their native habitat. Alas, it was discovered that the conversational repertoire of the largemouth bass is limited in the extreme.

For Lovers of Great Literature and Oratory . . .

The boy stood on the burning deck,
When the phone rang down below;
Through smoke and flame
He braved his way,
Picked it up and said,
HELLO?

A phone answer for those fond of quoting Shakespeare . . .

A slip of the foot
    You may soon recover
But a slip of the tongue
    You may never get over.
So watch it,
Buster.

I come from haunts
    Of coot and hern.
I've spoken.
    Now it is your turn.

Problems, Problems, Problems . . .

Do you have a problem? Of course you do. These phone answers may not solve your problem, but they are well calculated to earn you commiseration and sympathy . . .

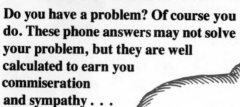

In answering your phone call,
Please don't think me brash
If I ask to borrow five dollars.
I'm in desperate need of cash.

What are you wishing
    To discuss?
Speak fast, I have to change
    My truss.

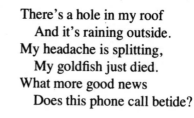

There's a hole in my roof
    And it's raining outside.
My headache is splitting,
    My goldfish just died.
What more good news
    Does this phone call betide?

Every little breeth
Theems to whithper Looeth,
Ever thinth I got
Thith new thet of teeth.

Speak to the point
And do not waffle
How're you feeling??
I'm just awful.

Are you my lost dog,
    Cutie Pup?
If you're not
    Then please hang up.

Bye baby bunting,
    Father's gone a-hunting,
And I'm left here all alone,
    Talking into this dumb phone.

79

The preceding problem-oriented phone answers didn't cover your particular dilemma? Fear not! Here are three more moving answers designed to reveal the mess you've gotten yourself into . . .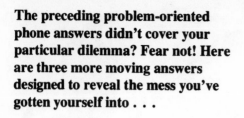

A suitable phone answer if you feel you may be under investigation by the CIA or FBI . . .

In confidence you may now confide,
   Most confidentially.
Unless they may have tapped my phone.
   Who knows? Well, not me!

My cat is in the sandbox,
   My husband's in the biffy.
What are you into, my friend?
   Please tell me in a jiffy.

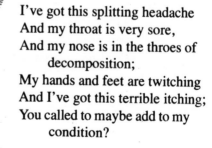

I've got this splitting headache
And my throat is very sore,
And my nose is in the throes of
   decomposition;
My hands and feet are twitching
And I've got this terrible itching;
You called to maybe add to my
   condition?

Before Rodney Pole invented the line-carrying upright, the telephone company hired men (unemployed wrestlers and CPAs, mostly) to hold up the phone lines.

**Phone answers
that reflect an abiding
conviction that telephones
actually exist,
and extolling the manifold
advantages thereof . . .**

An ingenious young fellow
    named Hugh,
Kept a telephone in his left shoe.
    He said, "It's sure neat,
    I can hear with my feet!
And my big toe can say
    'Howdy Do!'"

You don't have to know how to
    spell big words,
    You don't have to know how
    to write,
In order to make a telephone call.
    Is that why you phoned
    me tonight?

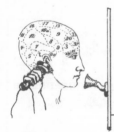

From the halls of Montezuma
To the shores of Tripoli,
It's possible now to dial direct.
Is that what you've done to me?

A phone call is fast and easy
You can call from most anyplace
And another nice thing about it
I don't have to look at your face.

82

Let Us Have Mercy and Forbearance

Professor Emile Chevalier in 1906 invented a combination telephone-hair dryer; the dryer worked only if the force of the incoming conversation was strong enough to create a hot wind. Wind suppressors are built into all modern telephones in order to avoid friction with the barber supply industry.

A phone answer evidencing the fact that you are possessed of a commendable religious tolerance . . .

> Christian, Muslim,
>   Shinto, Jew;
> I'll be glad
>   To talk with you.

An answer revealing a commendable absence of sexist prejudice . . .

> I'm ready to hear
> The sounds of your voice,
> Whether it is
> A girl's or a
> Boice.

An answer that indicates your tolerance extends even beyond the human species . . .

> I'm grasping the phone
>   And I'm ready to listen
> So if you're a snake
>   You may start your hissin'.

Phone answers employing Mother Bellinguistics . . .

This is not a recording,
You're hearing me live!
And I wait for the sound
Of your voice to arrive.

You have reached the resident
With whom you now may speak.
You're connected with the occupant
Whom you sought to seek.
I'm the human creature person
You've chosen now to phone,
So I'm prepared to listen now
To you, and you alone.

The number you have tried to
    reach
Is now in operation.
And you are free to talk with me,
So start the conversation.

The number you have tried
    to reach
Is not disconnected,
And this is no recording,
As you may have suspected.
So hello already!

A phone answer indicating a preference for another method of communication . . .

A phone call's fast,
But it don't last.
So maybe a letter
Might be better.

An editorial reply phone answer to the foregoing . . .

If you wrote me a letter
Instead of this call,
It might not make it
Here at all.
Mail, it sometimes
Takes a month!
But your telephone call
Got here at wunth.

THE TELEPHONE DRUMMER GIRLS
In the early days of the telephone, the ad agency believed the most efficient way to summon people to the phone was by a smart "rat-a-tat-tat," played on a snare drum. The telephone company thus employed many nattily-dressed drummer girls. But players of string and wind instruments picketed telephone company offices, protesting discrimination. To avoid altercations, the company developed the mechanical bell which remains in use even unto this day.

Milestones in Telephone History

Introduced during the reign of Ramses 654–9436, the Sarcophagus Phone made it possible—in theory, at least—for one to call home to Mummy.

Phone answers to or from people named Auntie Boo, Izzy, Moe, Morris, Johnson and rulers of Middle East Republics . . .

Is this Izzy, Moe or Morris?
Sing me now your verse and chorus.

If you called to ask
For Auntie Boo,
She died last week.
What else is new?

I'm the Sheik
Of Araby;
What is it that
You want of me?

My name is Yon Yonson,
I come from Wisconsin,
Where we make the good cheese in
the fall;
My phone it went yingle
And then dingle dingle,
So Yeezus Crise, why did you call?

87

A phone answer which may be personalized by simply inserting one's own name where the blank line appears. (If not sure what last name is, check phone directory.)

This isn't Dooley,
It isn't Gilhooley,
Instead you are speaking
To yours truly,

_____

A winter phone answer . . .

If your words are nice and warm
   I'll find that very pleasing,
Because it's very cold out here
   And my telephone is freezing.

It snowed on the trees in the village,
It snowed on the stones in the street,
It snowed through the hole in my
      outhouse roof,
And I'm frozen here to the seat.

And one for a summer day . . .

I hope your words are nice and cool,
   I hope that they're not icky.
Its a hundred in the shade now
   And this phone is hot and sticky.

Phone answers that reveal your healthy curiosity, coupled with your eagerness for news and information . . .

Twinkle, twinkle,
Little star!
How I wonder
Who you are!
So whether you
Are far or near,
Tell it to me
In my ear.

I hope your sick horse is better now, Joe.
When will you pay me the money you owe?
Why are you phoning at this hour of night?
Do you have free tickets for tomorrow's bullfight?

Tickle me
    With titillation,
Tell me now
    Your asservation.

What's the rubbish?
What's the rot?
What's the good word
That you've got?

GREAT PHONE BOOTHS OF HISTORY #162

The Bathaphone

A combined shower bath and public phone was promoted early in the century, with the slogan, "Cleanliness is next to Godliness and a pay telephone." After depositing 10¢, a person could make a 3 minute local call, as a bar of soap dropped from the coin return, and the shower head at the top of the booth became activated.

When does a baby awaken?
    In the wee-wee hours of the morn!
Even if you're not a farmer,
    You may now shuck your corn.

I'm listening
    With ears alert,
So you may start
    To dish the dirt.

I'm sitting here now
    All a-quiver
To hear the message
    You deliver.

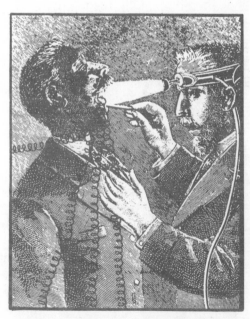

As sword swallowing waned in public popularity, The Great Rupert became the first man to swallow telephones before live audiences. Here a Philadelphia doctor examines the Great Rupert, during an appearance, to make sure all is well.

**A phone answer encouraging
self-reliance . . .**

This number in the
    Book is listed;
I hope you called it
    Unassisted.

**An appropriate answer if you have an
unlisted number . . .**

Since this number
    Isn't listed,
Howja know
    That it existed?

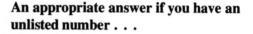

An answer for cliché lovers . . .

Hey, what's cookin'?
    What's for kicks?
What's new, fella?
    How is tricks?

**A phone answer ideal for anyone
proficient in playing the kazoo . . .**

Please do not speak
   Until you hear
The sound of
   The kazoo.
After you hear
   Its lovely tone,
I'll listen,
   Just to you.

(Now render brief kazoo interlude.)

**Two phone answers utilizable at
virtually any time and on any
occasion . . .**

I will listen
   To your utterance,
Then I'll give you
   My rebutterance.

Speak briefly
   If you wish;
Don't speak whale,
   Just small fish.

Vo do de oh!
   Boop boop a doo!
This is me!
   Who are you?

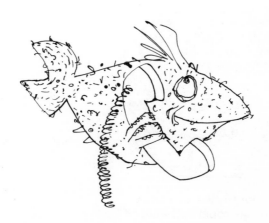

A phone answer enabling one to exude warmth and hospitality by inviting the caller to dinner, at a time you prefer the invitation will not be accepted . . .

Would you like to come over to dinner?
   I'm cooking the lettuce right now!
I got the soup in the bathroom to cool,
   And Wilma is wining the cow.
Our cow eats nothing but Concord grapes
   So instead of milk, she gives wine.
The entree tonight is cold oatmeal with fish,
   Would you like to come over to dine?

The first ads prepared by the ad agency
hinted that telephones could help ward off
crocodiles. Subsequent market research
showed other appeals to be more
effective.

A fitting phone answer for piscatorially-pointed persons . . .

I've been fishing all morning,
Since twenty minutes to nine;
I think I've finally got a bite,
So will you please hold the line?

Please listen carefully
  For the sound of the fish;
When you hear its piscine cadences
  You may say what you wish.

(Now imitate fish sounds.)

Note: The auditory manifestations of fish may vary according to depth, current, pollution, number of fishermen in the area and other factors. Among the more common sounds made by fish are *urk urk, oogle oogle* and *roooooop*, the latter having a rising inflection.

"Sacajawea Directing Lewis & Clark to the Nearest Phone Booth"

This remarkable fresco by Flora Wentworth Poltroon, grandfather of the author, now hangs in the Preserved Meat section of the Food Roundup in West Yellowstone, Montana.

The Phony Phone Book presents

The Yellow Pages!

INCREDIBLY SPLENDID CONTENTS:

- Exclusive pictures of the World's Foremost Yellow Things!
- Fantastic ads you won't find in ordinary yellow pages!
- Phictitious Phirm Names you may use for your own phone answering purposes!

When your phone rings, try answering it by reciting any of these names as they appear in our swell Yellow Pages. Or improve them by tacking on your very own true name! EXAMPLE: "The Home for the Morally Depraved" gains stature if you make it "The Edna Rasputin Home for the Morally Depraved." But if by some freak chance your name isn't Edna Rasputin, change it accordingly. Or you may prefer to append your actual genuine name to the tail end of names listed, like "Chicken Droppings, Unlimited—Edna Rasputin speaking."

Advertising Agencies

The Fake Snake Advertising
Agency   555-0123

FRENCH MASSAGE ADVERTISING AGENCY

"Service with a Smile"
Spinal Adjustments
Outcalls Kickbacks   555-2013

Housebroken Dog Ad Agency   555-3201

The Squirting Lapel Pin
Advertising Agency   555-1230

S & M AD SHOP
Sado-Masochistic Advertising   555-0213

Strayne & Grunnt

Consternation Consultants
555-0321

SUFFER FOOLS GLADLY
AD AGENCY
"Eventually—
Why Not Now?"
555-0312

Wripoff & Wrunn, Inc.
"Commission Magicians!"
555-0231

Airlines

AIRBORNE BROOMSTIX
"The Bewitching Airline"
555-3102

BEDPAN AM
"Convenience is our Watchword"
555-3012

Cow Over the Moon Airservice 555-3210
Darius Green Air   555-3201

FLY FCA
Flying Chicken Airlines   555-3100

Hang Glider International   555-3021
Mother's Cookie & Airline Co. 555-2031

THE WORLD'S FOREMOST YELLOW THINGS (#89)
Yellow dog inadvertently knocks over jar of mustard on
The Yellow Brick Road.

THE WORLD'S FOREMOST YELLOW THINGS (#117)
Yellow cab, filled with Hubbard squash, sinks in the Yellow Sea.

FLY PIE IN THE SKY AND SAVE!

Our flight crews pay US while they learn—so we have NO PAYROLL and pass the savings on to YOU. It's always exciting to fly

PIE IN THE SKY AIR 555-2130

PGA
Permanently Grounded Air 555-2301

TWI
Trans Wretched International 555-2103

FLY UDA
Unscheduled Destinations Airlines

Fly OUTSIDE and breathe FRESH AIR!

555-0011

UEL
United Emergency Landings 555-1100

U-FLY-IT
INTERNATIONAL
"Save with Self Service" 555-1010

Wing & Prayer Air 555-0110

Antiques

MAKE YOUR OWN ANTIQUES!

Rent our trained termites, carpenter ants, worms! Convert your out-dated new furniture to conversation-piece antiques!

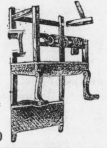

555-5430

Nixon Krakks, Unlimited 555-1111
Senile Sideboards 555-2222
Splittum, Crackem & Wormhole
"Engaging Aging" 555-3333

Artists

Your portrait rendered in chicken gravy!

CHICKEN ART, INC.
555-4444

Artists

LEONARDO, RAFAEL & DINO
Italian Masterpieces to Order

555-5555

REMBRANDT SALAD
Masterpieces rendered in oil and vinegar   555-6666

Undetectable Forgeries, Inc.   555-7777

Attorneys

Ambulance Pursuers, Inc.   555-8888

Boopboop, Dittum, Dottum,
Wattum & Chew   555-9999

JIGGERY POKERY ASSOCIATES   555-0000
"Lighting the Labyrinths of Litigation"

Malice, Grudge & Spleen   555-1122
Smirk, Snitch & Kurldlipp   555-2211

"No Suit Too Small"

Snide, Snitch & Snoop   555-1212

Automobile Dealers
—See Bullshippers

Beauty Salons

SAY GOODBYE TO STRINGY HAIR!

Always envied the luxurious, silky hair of the moose? Thanks to **Dr. Poltroon's Miracle Moose Oil,** lovely moosey locks can be yours!

DR. POLTROON'S MIRACLE MOOSE OIL   555-3330

THE WORLD'S FOREMOST YELLOW THINGS (#12)
Taiwan natives subdue a ferocious lion by inundating it
with warm chicken gravy.

Bicycles

**More fun on a
Mama's Moped!**

Mama's Mopeds   555-3303

Boats-Excursion

Fun & Jollies on an Albino Whale Hunt!

**Captain
Ahab's
Party Boats**   555-4201

CHARON'S PARTY BOATS

Floats down the River Styx

555-1024

Boat Repair

Don't go near the water without an Ormly Gumfudgin Emergency Boat Repair Kit!

Corks to Fit Every Size Hole
Gumfudgin Enterprises 248-5251

Bullies

FEAR MUGGERS NO MORE!

Learn how to cope with muggers—through 1st hand experience! When you subscribe to our service, our trained bullies subject you to armed robbery, senseless beatings, rape and junk mail.

MUGGERS DAY   555-0421

LIVE TV IN YOUR HOME

Let our staff of hardened criminals and hit men enliven your party! Ungovernable violence leaves your guests with unforgettable memories.   555-4102

THE WORLD'S FOREMOST YELLOW THINGS (#219)
Detective Charlie Chan, stricken with yellow fever, nevertheless summons
strength to attend the premiere performance of "Yellow, Dolly!"

Locked out

of your house? Or someone else's house? Call us! We break in anywhere.

24 hour service.

HOUSEBREAKERS, INC.

555-4201

Breath-Powered Weapons

YUCCH, INC.

Blowguns   Peashooters
Filibusters   Fresh garlic   555-4210

Buggy Whips

Giddyap Old Paint   555-4021
Horse Handles Unlimited   555-4012

Bunabs

GENUINE BUNABS

No Moving Parts to get out of order! Orville K. Snav's often-imitated, never-duplicated aid to nicer living can help you climb up out of the Muck & Meyer! Bunabs, $3 each mailed in PLAIN WRAPPER.

ORVILLE K. SNAV & ASSOC

Snav Towers, Mason City, Iowa 50401

515-423-2142

Cardsharps

–See Automobile Dealers, Used

Chiropractors

Maul, Yank & Pound   555-0011
Toebone, Heelbone, Fishbone &
   Trombone   555-5001

Cleaners

Ed's Edulcorators   555-5010

Salvation for your Filthy Things

HOPE THROUGH SOAP 555-5100

Meyer's Muck Movers

"Take Your Muck to Meyer"

555-5120

PIGEON SMUDGEON ERADICATORS

"Let us clean your soiled statuary"

555-6034

Costermongers

**CABBAGES
    SCALLIONS
ONIONS
    STRING BEANS
(NO BANANAS)**

Joe Costermonger   555-9000

THE WORLD'S FOREMOST YELLOW THINGS (#399)
Midgets wear bananas in their ears to alleviate yellow jaundice,
as they gather the yellow rose of Texas.

Crocodiles

Turns ordinary pools into exciting conversation pieces!

IT'S A CROC!   555-9888

Cretins

—See Bureaucrats and Politicians

Clothing-Men's

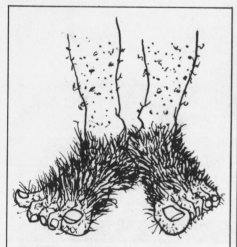

NEVER BUY SHOES AGAIN!

Apply liquid Natur-Shoo to your feet! In 2 days they're covered with luxurious fur! Choose from brown, black or saddle oxford! Easy upkeep: just wash feet once weekly (oftener if you live in muddy area).

DR. POLTROON'S NATUR-SHOO   555-6304

Our new GO APE shoes force you to walk **naturally**-on your hands **and feet**! When man started to walk upright (unnatural!), his troubles began! **Walk in peace, on all fours, in new**

GO APE SHOES   555-6340

WHY ARE PIGEONS SO HAPPY?

Because of the way they walk! New Pigeon Shoes slant your toes INWARD, make you walk the natural way pigeons do. *Wear Pigeon Shoes and get happy!*

PIDGE SHOES   555-6501

Clothing-Women's

Gowns for Shotgun Weddings
CHEZ BETS   555-6105

THE WORLD'S FOREMOST YELLOW THINGS (#33)
Proud bird with a yellow tail alights on a field of poached egg
yolks, as the golden sun sinks slowly in the west.

THE WORLD'S FOREMOST YELLOW THINGS (#541)
As the golden sun rises in the east, yellowfin tuna ascend the falls of the
Yellowstone River.

Clothing-Women's

THE FOUNDATION SHOP
Shoring & Underpinning   555-6234

"Let us respangle your tutu"

555-8900

MISS FATSO'S

Mini-Figleaf Fashions   555-6243

Contractors-Building

Jimkrax & Baling Wire   555-6324
Three Little Pigs Home
  Building   555-6342

Contractors-Electrical

The Blown Fuse   555-6432
Frayed Cord Electricians   555-6423
Socket To Me   555-6534

Cosmetics

Night In The Swamp
Parfum & Cologne
Eau de East River

FUMIGATION & FRAGRANCES
555-6543

Diaries

MARY'S DIARIES

"Our Cows Are Outstanding in their Fields"

555-6554

Dentists

"A flashing smile is always yours!"

NEON-GLO FILLINGS

(Batteries not included)
DR. BASCOM   555-6453

$AVE ON DENTAL BILLS!

Learn how to INTIMIDATE dentists! Make them AFRAID to hurt or overcharge!

TRANSCEND DENTAL MEDICATION

555-6354

NO PAIN
We immerse your entire head in gin while we drill, also when you pay your bill. Why suffer?

WINCE & QUAYLE, Dentists   555-6345

Daddies

Long Legs	555-8080
Sugar	555-0808
Warbucks	555-8800

Dingalings

—See Bureaucrats

Doctors

Butch Cassidy, M.D.	555-7534
Hopalong Cassidy, M.D.	555-7534
Perspi Cassidy, M.D.	555-7534

NO NO, NOSE!

"Let me stop your runny nose!"
Dr. Corkum   555-7543

DR. GEORGE CUSTER

Scalp Restoration

555-7435

ELECTRIC ORGAN TRANSPLANTS

Dr. Dingleberry   555-7543

OPTICAL ALEUTIANS

Eskimo Eye Doctors   555-7345

ELBOWS REMOVED!

Eat in comfort on airlines at last! Enjoy new freedom with total arm length of 10 inches!

DR. QUACKENBUSH   555-8430

DRS. SCHIZO & FREENIK

Wart transplants   555-8403

LEARN VOODOO ACUPUNCTURE!

Say goodbye to problems with neighbors, in-laws, etc.! With Voodoo Acupuncture Kit, you make dolls of up to 12 people. Complete with 1000 pins, chart of fatal areas of the human body, instructions.

DR. SCHMIDT   555-8403

Drilling

Let us drill for oil, gas, etc., in your bathroom!

Priceless gas, oil—who knows what?—may be directly beneath your bathroom! **Get rich overnight!** You provide bathroom, snacks and beer—we do the rest, split 50/50 on all producing wells.

JOHN DRILLERS   555-8034

THE WORLD'S FOREMOST YELLOW THINGS (#84)
Tibetan monks flee from persecution across a field of giant dandelions,
disguised as lemon popsicles to escape detection.

113

THE WORLD'S FOREMOST YELLOW THINGS (#1,239)
Angry goldfish about to repulse swarm of yellow jackets as they attack box of baking soda.

Entertainment

HEY FELLOWS!

Want to learn
all about girls?
Avoid guesswork,
get the FACTS.
We send you a
21 year old girl to
keep for a WHOLE WEEK!

LULU'S BACK IN TOWN
555-8034

Polly Wally Doodle
All Day & Night   555-8043
Wallow in Sin, Unlimited   555-8340

Escort Services

Dirty Old Man Escorts   555-8304
Lechers International   555-0987

Exterminators

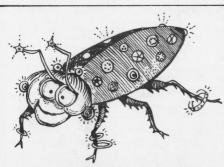

SAY GOODBY TO UGLY COCKROACHES!

Send for our Cockroach Improvement Kit!
Includes sequins, feathers, beads,
glue—everything you need to turn ugly
cockroaches into **beautiful household pets!**

THE KUDDLY KOCKROACH
555-0978

Fat Folks

OLD MOTHER BLUBBER
Fat people supplied for your
banquets and barbecues   555-0879

RENT A FATTIE!

Fill those cold empty spaces in your home
or office! Get needed extra weight over the
rear wheels of your pickup! Block unused
entrances to your home! *Hundreds of uses
for our fat people!*

RENT-A-FATTIE   555-0897

Food Manufacturers

Alexander Graham Cracker Co. 555-0798
Billy Graham Cracker Co.   555-0789
FILLERS & ADDITIVES
   Specializing in Natural Plastic
   Preservatives   555-1456

Food Manufacturers

The Lumpy Gravy Co.   555-1465

MOTHERS
Fruit Cake & Motorcycle Repair
555-1645

Organic Chocolate Sauerkraut   555-1654

BEFORE

AFTER

THE PICKLE DERMATOLOGISTS

We Remove the Warts
555-1664

Substandard Industries   555-1564
Unstrung Spaghetti Co.   555-2430

Food-Retail

NIPPONESE FISH & MEAT CO.

*Specializing in Sony Baloney
& Origami Salame*
555-2403

BUY LEFTOVER COFFEE FROM TV COMMERCIALS AND $AVE!

Oceans of fresh-brewed coffee go down the drain after TV commercials are filmed! **Now it's yours at big savings!** Articles dropped by movie stars—dental plates, jewels, money, etc.—easily strained out.

MRS. OLSEN'S BARGAIN BASEMENT
555-3340

Foundations

Prune Liberation League   555-2034

Fertilizer

–See also Automobile Dealers

CHICKEN DROPPINGS, UNLIMITED
"Mature Manure"
555-4251

MOOSELTOE
Organic Christmas
Tree Decor

*"A breath of Alaska
in your home"*

MR. MOOSEMAN
Box 1262 Homer, Alaska
555-4152

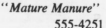

THE WORLD'S FOREMOST YELLOW THINGS (#101)
In West Yellowstone, Montana, the Knights of the Yellow Snow conduct a ritual burning of works of yellow journalism perpetrated by author Milford Poltroon.

117

THE WORLD'S FOREMOST YELLOW THINGS (#203)
The insidious Dr. Fu Manchu smuggles contraband eggnog across the
Yellow River.

Furnishings

Supersonic speeds are yours on your new

CONCORDE SKATEBOARD   555-4125

HONEST JOHNS
Trustworthy Restrooms   555-4512

LEARN THE SECRETS OF THE SWAMP!

Hundreds of nature's creatures—bugs, snakes, lizards, frogs, etc.—thrive in swamps! What's their secret? MUD! Mud is full of rich, nutritious INGREDIENTS! And without INGREDIENTS, man cannot grow and prosper! Let us build a genuine Muddi-Swamp in your home or pool!

MUDDI-SWAMPS, INC.   555-4521

HAPPY HOT TUB!

Our hot tubs hold up to 37 people!
Save on water, soap—put the FUN back in bathing! Free towel with every installation!
Snug Bug Rug Co.   555-5403

Garden Supplies

TAXES TOO HIGH?

Watch them drop, **drop, DROP,** when we replace your lawn & garden with natural crabgrass, foxtails and poison ivy! Low upkeep cost, easy to care for!

CRABGRASS FARMS   555-5403

EVIL WEEVILS

Let us consume your excess cotton
555-5034

Hobgoblins

FRED & ROY
Call us for all your Hobgoblin needs
FRED & ROY HOBGOBLIN
555-7070

Hotels

Holiday Septic Tank	555-5043
Pandemonium Condominiums	
	555-5304
Sheriton Gravel Pit	555-9430
The Wiltin'Hiltin	555-9403

Income Tax

Certified Public Klutzes	555-9034
High Dudgeon Tax Service	555-9043

Incompetents

ARE YOU GETTING YOURS?

Government and business firms today are filled with dumbbells, incompetents. DO YOU HAVE YOUR SHARE? Mistakes help humanize your firm—*nobody likes a smartass!*

MISFITS, INC.

555-8501

Insurance
–See also under Cardsharps

Bowl of Cherries Life Underwriters	555-8510
Mutual Disagreement	555-8105
Rock of Milpitas Life	555-8015
Trepidation International	555-8051

UNMITIGATED CATASTROPHES
Accident & Life   555-8150

Itinerants
–See Tramps, Loafers and Wastrels

Jugglers
–See Income Tax Preparation

Jungles
–See Ghettos

TARZAN'S CONDOS

Live in a tree and save on taxes

555-7771

Mountain Climbing

LEARN MOUNTAIN CLIMBING BY MAIL!

Learn how to go up walls *in your own home*—then trees, elevator shafts, phone poles, etc. Advance to Coping with Mountain Goats, 27 Tasty Ways to Cook Snow, How to Deabominablize Snowmen

UP THE WALL, INC.   555-1110

Music

IVORIES BY THE YARD
Custom-built pianos with up to 375 keys instead of the dull, ordinary 88   555-1112

Nasal Flautists Association   555-1113

Pets

Own an EAGER BEAVER!

Trained to eat parking meters (rich in iron), attack on command!

EAGER BEAVERS, INC. 555-1115

THE WORLD'S FOREMOST YELLOW THINGS (#2)
Milford ("Stanley") Poltroon, known to his intimates as "Old Yellowbelly," is
freely acknowledged to be the world's leading coward.

Pets

FROGONIANS
Ribet & Kneedeep   555-0291

Stop paying high prices for milk, yogurt, ice cream! Let your rented cow do the job and **$AVE!** You get endless supply of fresh dairy products, PLUS energy-saving lawn mower, organic fertilizer and a lovable pet for the kiddies!

HURTZ RENT-A-COW   555-1117

Own a Pet Moose!

"Man's Best Friend"

THE MOOSALEUM   555-1118

THE HAPPY HIPPO

A clean hippopotamus is a happy hippopotamus. We specialize in sanitizing hippopotamus and walrus.

HIPPO SHOWER & SAUNA
555-1119

Phrenologists

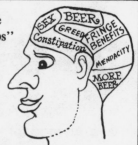

"Learn to live by your lumps"

Dr. Wetley P. Bedford
555-9210

Plumbing

WE PIPE ANYTHING TO YOUR HOME
Omni-Pipe brings chicken soup, shaving cream, beer, gravy, disinfectant and gin *DIRECT TO YOUR HOME!* Just dial your choice, in your bathroom or kitchen, turn the faucet—*OUT IT COMES!*

THE ROYAL PIPERS   555-1120

Religious

Little Chapel of the Praying Mantis	555-1121
Holy Mackerel Fish Market & Chapel	555-1122

Restaurants

THE BATEATERY
**Take out food for vampires
and werewolves**

555-1133

THE BOILED SHOE

Specializing in food JUST LIKE
MOTHER USED TO MAKE when she
worked as a night watchman at the
garbage processing plant   555-1134

THE FOOT LOCKER CAFE
"You'll go for our Gopherburgers"

555-1136

DINO'S UPSTAIRS BASEMENT
*A subsidiary of Luigi's
Downstairs Attic*   555-1135

Retirement Homes

God's Waiting Room	555-1138
Heaven's Doorstep Manor	555-1139
Senility Acres	555-1140

Schools

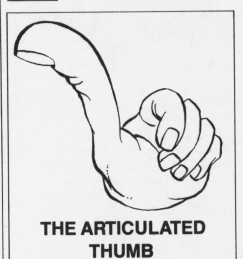

THE ARTICULATED THUMB

Lessons in Hitch-hiking   555-1141

OFF THE GROUND, INC.
Learn plastic making and
airline food preparation.   555-1142

GERIATRIC THEATRICS
Learn to act your age

555-1143

EAT AT THE HORSE CAFE

"You'll whinny for more!"

555-1137

A One Gun Salute to Mother Bell

I grew up in a small town nobody every heard of, named Utica, Pennsylvania. (Now you've heard of it.) When I was a kid, the four principal forms of communication in Utica were yelling, stuffing notes in bottles to throw in French Creek, writing letters and making telephone calls.

Yelling was the cheapest and often the most effective. Good yellers could be heard easily three blocks away. Since Utica was only two blocks long (measured diagonally), yelling was a favorite communication method back then. Floating bottles containing notes down French Creek was fun, and sometimes months later (almost as long as it takes mail today), you might get a reply, by phone or mail, from some eccentric many miles down the Allegheny River, into which French Creek flowed.

Since those distant years, both bottling and yelling messages have fallen out of favor. Jet aircraft, motorcycles and all those people eating potato chips make it hard for anyone to hear you, no matter how hard you yell. (1948 saw the last Olympic Yelling Teams in action.) And floating bottled notes downstream is a bummer, because it's all one way: in 1948 scientists discovered that bottles won't float upstream very far. So that leaves writing letters and telephoning. And how have they fared since the turn of the century?

Well, back in 1900 you could send a letter anywhere in the U.S.A. for 2¢. And a postcard needed only a penny stamp. Airmail didn't cost extra, mainly because airplanes hadn't yet been satisfactorily invented. So it might take as long as ten days for a letter to make it from Boston to San Francisco. But it always got there eventually. Local delivery almost never took more than 24 hours. People who worked for the post office back then were friendly, courteous and efficient. I know because my Uncle Horatio was one of them. And he told me so. And my Uncle Horatio would never lie to you.

But at the same time the post office was cooking on all its burners, the telephone company was suffering from growing pains. A local call for under a minute usually cost at least a quarter, big money in those days. In 1908, you could buy a pair of first-rate men's or ladies' leather shoes from Sears Roebuck for $1.49; kids' shoes were under 50¢. Only rich folks could afford long distance calls. If you lived in San Francisco, for example, and wanted to gossip with Aunt Minnie, up there in Spokane, a 15 second call would cost you $1. What could you say in just 15 seconds? Phone directories of that era obligingly provided a recommended script, as follows:

> YOU CAN EASILY transmit 30 words in ¼ of a minute! Try the following: "I did not telegraph, fearing you were out of town. Could not spare the time to go upon the train. Must have your decision now, so called you by telephone."

No one, then or since, ever actually talked that way. And if you insisted on yakkity-yakking for more than 15 seconds, you paid an extra $3 for every additional minute or fraction thereof.

In the beginning years of this century, it was par for the course to wait thirty minutes or more, while the telephone operators made all the complex connections between San Francisco and Spokane. And when you finally did get Aunt Minnie, she sounded like she was talking from the bottom of a deep hole, with popcorn cooking all around her.

The letter you mailed for two cents back then now requires 15¢ —unless they've upped it even more since these words were written. And it often takes much longer for it to reach its destination (optimistically assuming it ever does!) than it did in 1900. And when you complain to the post office, you're seldom greeted with the friendliness and courtesy of Uncle Horatio's day.

Contrariwise, the telephone company has improved service 3 jillion percent, in the same time period. The San Francisco-Spokane call that set you back $4 for 1¼ minutes back in 1900 now costs you $2.10 for a full three minutes, and in reduced rate time periods, even less. (In one minute, name as many things as you can that cost less today than they did fifty or seventy five years ago.) And the once common-place static is but a raspy memory; a call from Seattle to London today is even more clear and crackle-free than yelling was fifty years ago in Utica, Pa. Wrong numbers, once par for the course, are now exceedingly rare: If you do get one, it's usually your own fault—automated systems of the phone company seldom make mistakes.

This isn't to say the phone company is without fault. There's a public phone I use, half a mile up in the woods from my Montana cabin. Half the time it's out of order, usually because beavers prefer the telephone cable to pine and aspen for making their dams. It seems to me the phone company could make less tasty wire, if they put their minds to it. And pay phones in the closest village have an eccentric habit of sometimes not returning your coin when you fail to complete your call. Compensatingly, though, at other times they shower you with dimes and nickels. There's one phone in West Yellowstone (I'm not saying where) that hardly ever fails to reward me with fifty or sixty cents, after I finish a call. Slot machines aren't legal here. With Mountain Bell's pay phones, who needs them?

I own no stock in AT & T, nor do I have any kinfolk laboring there. The foregoing is entirely uncoerced personal reflection. I do feel the phone company is deserving of a one gun salute, and here it is:

BANG

Milford ("Stanley") Poltroon
1979

I'm going to hang up now

Visitors to Yellowstone National Park may notice that Mountain Bell has thoughtfully provided the area with roving Public Meese, each equipped with a pay telephone. The moose antlers serve as an antenna, transmitting the call to a satellite or Bozeman.